Safari Sam's Wild Animals

Desert Animals

A⁺

Smart Apple Media

Published by Smart Apple Media, an imprint of Black Rabbit Books
P.O. Box 3263, Mankato, Minnesota 56002
www.smartapplemedia.com

Produced by David West Children's Books
6 Princeton Court, 55 Felsham Road, London SW15 1AZ

Designed and illustrated by David West

Cataloging-in-Publication Data is available from
Library of Congress
ISBN 978-1-62588-070-3

Printed in China
CPSIA compliance information: DWCB15CP
311214

9 8 7 6 5 4 3 2 1

Safari Sam says:
I will tell you something
more about the animal.

Learn what this animal eats.

Where in the world is the animal found?

Its size is revealed!

What animal group is it—mammal, bird, reptile, amphibian, insect, or something else?

Interesting facts.

Contents

Burrowing owl

Safari Sam says:
When threatened by a **predator,** burrowing owl chicks make a hissing noise that sounds like a rattlesnake.

Burrowing Owls

These small, long-legged birds live in grasslands and deserts. They make their nests underground in old burrows. The burrows have been dug out and abandoned by mammals, such as ground squirrels and prairie dogs.

Burrowing owls eat small mammals, such as moles and mice. They also eat insects including grasshoppers and beetles. The owls might also eat birds, amphibians, and reptiles.

Burrowing owls live in North America, South America, and the Caribbean islands.

Burrowing owls are about 10 inches (25.4 centimeters) tall and weigh about 5 ounces (0.15 kilograms).

Burrowing owls are members of the owl order of birds. Owls have flat faces and large eyes.

During the nesting season, burrowing owls leave animal dung around the burrow entrance to attract insects to eat.

Camels

Camels are well suited to life in the harsh conditions of a desert. They store most of their fat in their hump. Since fat keeps heat in, storing the fat in one place helps keep the rest of the camel's body cool. The camel's long legs keep its body away from the ground, which can reach 158 °F (70 °C).

Safari Sam says:
Some camels have two humps. They are called bactrian camels. A camel with one hump is called a dromedary camel.

Dromedary camel

Camels eat plants. They can eat thorny twigs without injuring their mouths.

Camels are found in the wild in Africa, the Middle East, Central Asia, and Australia.

A camel is 6.1 feet (1.9 meters) tall at the shoulder and 7 feet (2.1 meters) tall at the hump.

Camels are mammals. Mammals have fur and give birth to live young.

A camel can drink 53 gallons (200 liters) of water in one day.

Coyotes hunt rabbits, rodents, fish, frogs, and deer. They also eat insects, snakes, fruit, and grasses.

Coyotes are found in most of North America and parts of Central America.

Coyotes stand about 1.5 to 2 feet (0.5 to 0.6 meters) high and weigh from 15 to 50 pounds (7 to 23 kilograms).

Coyotes are mammals and members of the dog family.

Coyotes generally hunt at night, although they are sometimes seen during the day. They can run up to 40 mph (64 kph).

Coyote

Coyotes

Coyotes live in many **habitats,** such as deserts, prairies, forests, and mountains. Coyotes are known for their deep howl. They are clever animals and appear in folk tales as tricksters.

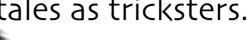

Safari Sam says:
Coyotes are smaller than wolves. Sometimes they are called prairie wolves or brush wolves. They are also known as the American jackal.

9

Fennec foxes mainly eat insects, small mammals, and birds.

The fennec fox is found in North Africa and Asia.

The fennec fox is the smallest fox at 12 to 16 inches (30 to 40 centimeters) long. Its huge ears alone measure about 5 inches (13 centimeters) long.

The fennec fox is a mammal and a member of the dog family.

The fennec fox has excellent hearing and can hear its prey moving underground.

Fennec fox

10

Desert Foxes

The fennec fox is a type of small desert fox found in the Sahara desert of North Africa and in the Arabian desert. Its large ears help rid its body of heat. The fox's ears also allow it to detect the movement of insects and small mammals when it hunts at night.

Safari Sam says:
Fennec foxes' feet are hairy, which protects them from extremely hot sand. The hair also softens the sound of their footsteps when they are hunting.

Desert Rats

Also known as desert rats, Mongolian gerbils have become popular pets. In the wild, they live in deserts and semi-desert regions in social groups. They look similar to field mice, but have a furry tail that is as long as their body.

Mongolian gerbils eat seeds of grasses and other plants and small insects, such as beetles.

The Mongolian gerbil originated in the semi-arid deserts of Mongolia. Other **species** can be found in India and Africa.

Mongolian gerbils are typically about 8 inches (20 centimeters) long.

Desert rats are mammals and members of the rodent order, which includes rats and squirrels.

Gerbils store fat in their bodies that can be converted to water during times of drought.

Mongolian gerbil

Safari Sam says:
Gerbils are hunted by birds of prey and snakes. To get away from these predators, they dive down into their burrows or jump long distances.

13

Gila Monsters

The Gila monster is a desert-dwelling lizard with a poisonous bite. They spend more than 90 percent of their time in underground burrows. They emerge to feed on eggs and baby mammals that they raid from nests.

Safari Sam says:
Although the Gila monster has a poisonous bite, it is very slow moving and is not a threat to humans.

Gila monster

The Gila monster feeds on small birds, mammals, frogs, lizards, and eggs.

The Gila monster is native to the southwest United States and to northwest Mexico.

The Gila monster grows to about 19 inches (48 centimeters) long. It weighs about 4 pounds (1.8 kilograms).

The Gila monster is a reptile.

The Gila monster stores fat in its stumpy tail and can go without food for months.

15

Hyenas

Hyenas have a reputation for being cowardly, but, in fact, can stand their ground against leopards and cheetahs. They are usually active at night and have been known to raid garbage piles.

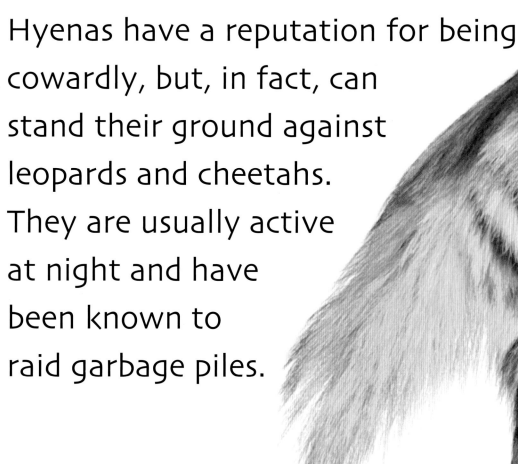

Safari Sam says:
Hyenas are often called "laughing hyenas" because their calls sound like a person laughing.

16

Striped hyena

Striped hyenas are mainly scavengers, but have been known to kill their own prey. They eat meat, insects, and fruit.

Hyenas live in Africa, the Middle East, and South Asia.

Hyenas vary in size, but many are about the size of a large dog at 3.5 feet (1 meter) long and weigh about 75 pounds (35 kilograms).

Hyenas are mammals. They are more closely related to cats than dogs, although they have doglike habits.

Hyenas have powerful jaws that can crush bones to get at the juicy marrow inside.

Scorpions

Scorpions are tough creatures that can survive the hot daytime temperatures in the desert sun. Though the cold night temperatures in the desert can fall to below freezing, scorpions hunt at night. They have a poisonous sting in their tails, which quickly kills their prey.

Scorpions mainly eat insects, but larger ones will also eat small mammals and lizards.

Scorpions are found in nearly every habitat, including mountains and jungles, but do not live in the polar regions or in water.

Most scorpions can grow from 0.5 to 8 inches (1.3 to 20 centimeters) long.

Scorpions are members of the **arachnid** family, which includes spiders. Arachnids have eight legs.

Female scorpions are good mothers. After her young are born, she carries them on her back until they are old enough to fend for themselves.

Safari Sam says:
Scientists have put scorpions in a freezer overnight to test the toughness of their bodies. When they took them out of the freezer the next morning, the scorpions thawed out and were able to walk away.

Scorpion

19

Tarantula

Safari Sam says:
Some tarantulas have mildly
venomous hairs on their
abdomens. They use their legs
to kick the hairs into the faces
of attacking animals.

Tarantulas

Tarantulas are large, hairy spiders that live in a variety of habitats. Most of them live in burrows made in the soil or desert sand. Tarantulas spin webs, but not for catching food. Instead, tarantulas ambush their prey, killing them with poison injected by their **fangs**.

Tarantulas mainly eat insects, but these spiders also eat bigger animals, such as frogs, lizards, birds, and mice.

Tarantulas of various species live in the southern United States, Central America, and South America. Other species occur in Africa, Asia, Australia, and in some parts of southern Europe.

The largest tarantula measures about 3 to 3.5 inches (7.6 to 8.9 centimeters) long. Its legspan can be more than 10 inches (25 centimeters) long.

Tarantulas are spiders and are members of the arachnid family.

Tarantulas inject venom, or poison, into their prey. The venom turns the prey into a liquid that the spider can suck up like soup.

Vultures

Vultures are large birds that feed on the **carcasses** of dead animals on deserts, plains, and mountains around the world. Vultures have excellent eyesight. They can often be seen high in the sky, gliding in circles and searching for their next meal.

Most vultures only eat meat.

Vultures are found in Africa, Asia, Europe, and in the Americas.

The griffon vulture can grow to 3 feet (1 meter) long with an 8.5-foot (2.6-meter) wingspan. They can weigh up to 25 pounds (11.3 kilograms). That's heavy for a bird!

Vultures are members of the bird class.

Vultures gorge themselves when food is plentiful. Sometimes they can become too heavy to take flight.

Safari Sam says:
Vultures have sharp beaks to rip meat from their prey's bones. With their long necks, they can reach deep into a carcass.

Griffon vulture

23

Glossary

arachnid
A group of animals that have an exterior skeleton and eight legs.

carcass
The body of a dead animal.

fangs
The biting mouth parts of a spider through which poison is injected.

habitat
The natural area where certain types of animals and plants live.

predator
An animal that hunts other animals for food.

species
A group of animals that have similar characteristics and can produce offspring.

Index